REDGROVE'S WIFE

Penelope Shuttle has lived in Cornwall since 1970, is the widow of the poet Peter Redgrove, and has a grown-up daughter Zoe, who works in the field of renewable energy.

Her first collection of poems, *The Orchard Upstairs* (1981) was followed by six other books from Oxford University Press, *The Child-Stealer* (1983), *The Lion from Rio* (1986), *Adventures with My Horse* (1988), *Taxing the Rain* (1994), *Building a City for Jamie* (1996) and *Selected Poems 1980-1996* (1998), and then *A Leaf Out of His Book* (1999) from Oxford Poets/Carcanet and *Redgrove's Wife* (2006) from Bloodaxe Books. First published as a novelist, her fiction includes *All the Usual Hours of Sleeping* (1969), *Wailing Monkey Embracing a Tree* (1973) and *Rainsplitter in the Zodiac Garden* (1977).

With Peter Redgrove, she is co-author of *The Wise Wound: Menstruation and Everywoman* (1978) and *Alchemy for Women: Personal Transformation Through Dreams and the Female Cycle* (1995), as well as a collection of poems, *The Hermaphrodite Album* (1973), and two novels, *The Terrors of Dr Treviles: A Romance* (1974) and *The Glass Cottage: A Nautical Romance* (1976).

Shuttle's work is widely anthologised and can be heard on The Poetry Archive Website. Her poetry has been broadcast on BBC Radio 3 and 4, and her poem 'Outgrown' was used recently in a radio and television commercial. She has been a judge for many poetry competitions, is a Hawthornden Fellow, and a tutor for the Poetry School. She is current Chair of the Falmouth Poetry Group, one of the longest-running poetry workshops in the country.

PENELOPE SHUTTLE

Redgrove's Wife

BLOODAXE BOOKS

10314482

ISBN: 1 85224 734 7

First published 2006 by
Bloodaxe Books Ltd,
Highgreen,
Tarset,
Northumberland NE48 1RP.

www.bloodaxebooks.com
For further information about Bloodaxe titles
please visit our website or write to
the above address for a catalogue.

Bloodaxe Books Ltd acknowledges
the financial assistance of
Arts Council England, North East.

Cover printing by J. Thomson Colour Printers Ltd, Glasgow.

Printed in Great Britain by
Bell & Bain Limited, Glasgow.

In memory of Peter and Dad,
and for Mum and Zoe

ACKNOWLEDGEMENTS

Acknowledgements are due to the editors of the following publications in which some of these poems first appeared: *Acumen, Ambit, Boomerang, Leviathan, The Manhattan Review, Mslexia, PN Review, Poetry Ireland, Poetry Kanto, Poetry London, Poetry Review, Poetry Wales, The Republic of Letters, The Rialto, Shearsman, The Shop, Stride, The Review of Contemporary Poetry, Thumbscrew, The Waterlog* and *The Wolf.*

'Wife, Widow' was awarded second prize in the Poetry-on-the-Lake Competition, 2004; 'Running Out of Time' was awarded second prize in the Renato Giorgi Competition, 2004.

Many thanks to the Hawthornden Foundation for a Fellowship in 2005, to the Royal Literary Fund for financial support during the writing of these poems, and to Michael Bayley and the Falmouth Poetry Group for their valued comments.

CONTENTS

The Songs

Choosing tears as a vocation
I saw the world as ghostly greens
and golds,

as coasts, as replicas of coasts,
as faint coincidences of the window

I wept my *Weltanschauung* in the deepest green kingdom
of young woods, in orchards
of the bystander nectarine

On a river three miles late
I saw the remaining marriages of swans

The songs I sang
when I went out with my father
shone with rubies and diamonds,

with beauty and history,
even after so long, after all those tears

Weltanschauung: world view.

Redgrove's Wife

Pity Redgrove's Wife?
I think not.

Praise Redgrove's Wife?
Why not?

Kiss n'snog Redgrove's Wife?
I dare not.

Be-jewel Redgrove's Wife?
With topaz and coral?
I will not.

Publish Redgrove's Wife?
I shall not.

(But I shall).

Forget Redgrove's Wife?
No, I have not.

Question Redgrove's Wife?
Not yet, not yet.

Confuse Redgrove's Wife?
I need not.

Fear Redgrove's Wife?
Oh fear not.

Dream of Redgrove's Wife?
Yes, night after night.

Translate Redgrove's Wife?
Why not,
she's not made of tin.

Amaze Redgrove's Wife?
Leave that to Redgrove.

Written as wedding anniversary poem for Peter two years before he died.

By the Water's Edge

By the flowing water's edge
Orpheus leads Eurydice
up out of the pit,

stepping fast
through a landscape of rocks and caves

The new moon blew her trumpet,
the sun shot up like a cedar in Lebanon

Too busy singing,
the singer did not look back

There

Rain woke up,
spread his peacock tail,
lifted his wondering head

Light and all his henchmen were there,
some wage-earning clouds also

The trees stowed away their leaves

Like a seraph, the willow lingered

I was there –
was September in the north,
a keepsake of the sun

I was there forever

To Be Whispered

Like an alphabet
refusing to breed in captivity

or a holy city
left out of history,

I scatter your ashes
in the autumn tide

I'm the moon continuing to grieve for you,
your gift to the children of France,

the fire that gives the world
fifty minutes to clear its museums of every Rembrandt

If I could choose,
I'd be happy at the foot of the page

If I was twilight,
or a cliff swallow, or one of those feline spiders
you loved,

I'd follow you in your new life
as salt water,

not return to the empty house
where nothing of you lingers,

summer
shut and barred behind you,

and begin once more
to draw pictures of your absence

till it seems you're right at my fingertips
if only I can work out how to touch you

The Breather Among the Metals

I hold the world's supply
         of quicksilver
                in my hands,
carry copper in my heart
         as a bird carries copper
                in its red feathers
I share gold's kinship with light,
         am often also
                gold's obedient half-sister,
or turn my glance to silver,
         a chemistry mirroring
                contradictions
I unfold the dynamics
         of topaz and tin,
                hinder the mischief of cobalt,
correct the vices of asbestos,
         ponder the leitmotif of lead,
                the crucial rainbows
of sulphur
         For I'm the breather
                among the metals,
my foundry inclines to you,
         making its own laws
                of upper, lower and middle
brightness
         Here are my forges
                and my spiral classifiers,
my old green schists,
         my weathered and exploited adamance,
                here are my helpers
and repairers,
         my precipitates and prisms,
                my alloys and resins,
my selfless antimony
         who deserves a chapter
                all to himself
I'm the breather among,
         I live everywhere
                even in nettles and yarrow

I colour the world
                  I'm with and for the light
                              I make plants green
and blood red
                  Even as cosmic dust
                              I'm always drifting down
to replenish my flasks,
                  those that are above the sun,
                              those that are below

'The breather among the metals': iron; Wilhelm Pelikan, *The Secrets of Metals* (Anthroposophic Press Inc, 1973).

In the Kitchen

A jug of water
has its own lustrous turmoil

The ironing-board thanks god
for its two good strong legs and sturdy back

The new fridge hums like a maniac
with helpfulness

I am trying to love the world
back to normal

The chair recites its stand-alone prayer
again and again

The table leaves no stone unturned
The clock votes for the separate burial of hearts

I am trying to love the world
and all its 8000 identifiable languages

With the forgetfulness of a potter
I'm trying to get the seas back on the maps
where they belong,

secured to their rivers

The kettle alone knows the good he does,
here in the kitchen, loving the world,
steadfastly loving

See how easy it is, he whistles

Running Out of Time

I was running out of time
or time was running out of me

I was no longer
decades of clear water

Time
was a cache of lions,
the end of all the birds

I was hurrying to catch up with Time,
while Time stayed home

doing the ironing,
folding his minutes,
smoothing his hours,

soon there'd be not a crumpled second
for me to hide in

Wife, Widow

Like any married woman
I dream of great houses
disabled by fire,

of maps that grow of themselves,
like old experiments
in organic chemistry

Like any widow
I have a garden
where twelve Apostles and a Christ

dine on mist and rain

Like any married woman
I rank myself below a queen,
above a princess

Like any widow
my rivers are bridged by chance,

I long for a world
where rain is still being invented

Like any wife
I've known doors to be only slightly open
and for no one to come through them

Like any widow
I'm as much use
as a second moon or a spare sun,

a thorn without a rose,
a nation without a bathhouse

Like any married woman
I'm the map of everywhere

Like any widow I honour the bloodstone,
revere the pearl

Like any wife
I'm the world's only cloud,
the speech for the defence

Like any widow
the rainbow is not enough for me,
nor is the flood

January is not enough, nor June
Jasmine is not enough,
nor the honeysuckle

Like any wife
I watch the blue of ideas
turning to green

Like any widow
I dream I'm with child,

forging a tiny suit of armour
for my newborn

Peter's Shoes

After a year,
I put your black shoes out
for the re-cycler

Two pairs

Our walks go with them,
our days out,
our journeys

In the red casket of the bin
they wait as if for you,
but you're as far away as Dad,

whose new widow
keeps his suede brogues
on guard in the glass porch

to scare off intruders

The Inattentive Reader
(Henri Matisse, Tate Modern)

I too am an inattentive reader,
lean my head on my hand,
like this girl who isn't reading her book

I also wait for answers
to my unpopular questions,
let time stand still beside me

Here are the girl's flowers,
her mirror, carpet,
and here is my room,

not so very different

Like her, I have things on my mind,
turn to the future as to a stranger,
to the past as to a friend

She's conducting a masterclass in reverie,
with her talent for not reading,
never losing the thread of her daydream

If I could, Peter,
my ever-attentive reader,
I'd paint your portrait

over an old *Flight into Egypt*,
build you a house out of Mondays and Thursdays,
a boat from Fridays and Wednesdays

But no house, portrait or boat
tempts you back to life,
and as a painter is never truly confused about colours

so you are clear in your mind about your death;
the slightest fever heals you,
the simplest rain lets you fall

Missing You

This year no one will ask how you voted,
or if you know the way to town

No one will call you as an eye-witness
or teach you how to train a bird of prey

No one will bring you your *New Scientist*,
try to sell you double-glazing
or tell you their secrets

People will write to you
but you won't answer their letters

The high sheriff of mistletoe
will never catch your eye again

No one will peel apples for you,
or love you more than you can bear

No one will forget you

2

I wept in Tesco,
Sainsburys
and in Boots

where they gave me
medicine for grief

But I wept in Asda,
in Woolworths
and in the library

where they gave me
books on grief

I wept in Clarks
looking in vain for shoes
that would stop me weeping

I wept on the peace march
and all through the war

I wept in Superdrug
where they gave me
a free box of tissues

I wept in the churches,
the empty empty churches,

and in the House of Commons –
they voted me out of office

3

I can't cry anyone's tears except my own,
can't teach anything but my own ignorance

I can only fall from my own mountain,
ledge by ledge

I can't rival the wasp's sting
or sew except with my needle

Like a saltwater wife,
I prise open the oyster of my loss,

hoick out the pearl of your death

4

The rainbow is not enough,
nor the flood

My eye can't see enough,
nor my ear absorb sufficient silence

January is not enough,
nor June

Books are not enough,
nor the El Grecos

Christianity is not enough,
nor Judaism

China is not enough,
nor India

Good luck is not enough,
nor absolution from the bad

Jasmine is not enough,
nor the rose

Kingdoms are not enough,
nor the oldest city in the world,

without you

5

I used to be a planet,
you discovered me

I used to be a river,
you travelled to my source

I used to be a forest,
you ran away to me

I used to be the sky,
you traipsed up mountains to touch me

I used to be a moon,
you saw by my light

I was hot coals,
you held me

I used to be an atom,
you split me

I was music,
you often sang me

6

Like a tough Polish soldier
you put your clean shirt on wet

Like a rainbow without red,
you troubled the sky

You were my sower sowing wide,
my queue dans la bouche

You loved top-knotted Islamic angels
with their steep wings of gold and blue

You preferred astronomer's weather,
sciences of the birds

You were a prayer across the Orinoco,
a Tiber fitting me to perfection

7

The sky knows everything about you
but won't tell

My questions vanish to the south-west

The sea knows something about you
but keeps silent,

my enquiries turned back on the tide

The moon knows all about you
but won't speak for a thousand years

The world, knowing all about you,
swings away on its axis,

not beating about the beautiful bush

I bide my time,
just as you warned me I would

8

I've forgotten everything
the sun and moon taught me

Perhaps they were not so wise

The world was so small
I hid it in my heart

like a woman pregnant
before she was born

I've forgotten what a painter of portraits
does with a brush,

what a musician does with tone and semi-tone,
what a gardener does with a seed,

forgotten that fire burns,
grief's disbelief never ends

9

Don't bring me the sea,
or clouds, or those packs of trees,
don't bring me night, or stars
or forthright moons, or the solitude
of the river; take away
that farmyard of cyclamen,
your flooded side-street, don't bring me
the sun, leave it where it is,
don't offer me operas or banknotes,

spider-webs peppered with dew –
I don't want a bullfight
or a cushion you've worked yourself –
I don't want anything except the past,
bring me five years ago, last winter,
the week before last, yesterday

10

I make my home in your absence,
take your smallest hope

and make it grow

I wake to the dusk of everywhere
as if assisting at my own birth

or arriving in a country
where all the rivers settle down to be ice

11

World was one word
I could not guess it

World was one gesture
I could not copy it

World was one question
I couldn't answer it

World was one song
How could I sing it?

World was one forest
I couldn't fell it

World was one bridge
How was I to cross it?

12

You're a tree's guess,
a cloud's confidence,

the continent of January,
the solitude of a comet,

a world without a wren

You're the heart of when,
the pulse of where,

sleepy as a motorway,
eager as an earthquake,

elusive as an elegy,
daring as dusk

You invent your own exit
via the black economy of poetry

13

My tamer of doves,
my alphabet of the moon,
fool of night,
harvest's welcome, the grief
of day, my blind man
and my seer,
dreamer against his will,
my furious saint,
warrior of peace

14

I won't find you in the featherbed of thought
or in the blip of the city

To find you I must be the bloodhound of love,
block capitals of the rain,

swift and slow at once,
because you'll be everywhere I'm not

Suddenly I'll be there beside you
as if all the time you'd been only four streets away

15

I'm the leopard changing my spots,
the horse led to water I must drink,

the elephant who forgets,
a silk purse sewn from the sow's ear

I'm the long long road with no turning,
the cloud without a silver lining

Mine is the last straw
that mends the camel's back,

sails us both
through the needle's effortless eye

16

Think of me
as a small backward country
appealing for aid from the far-off first world

Imagine the dirt of my shrines,
the riddle of my dry rivers,
the jinx of my cities

When you hold the full purse of autumn
or celebrate the nativity of a pear,

picture me as the hawk of spring,
a one-pupil school,
the safe-keeper of sunrise

Think of me without you,
stuck here forever between rainless May
and the drought of June

17

Your name didn't change
after your death –
many others also answered to it

After your death
the climate didn't change,
the government stayed calm

Waterfalls
remembered you forever,
remaining loyal,
looking for you everywhere,
storm after storm, teacup after teacup

18

Autumn fans its tail without you
and spring bears its burden alone

Summer, that small supernatural being,
manages without you

and winter closes your many doors

Like an interval between kings,
the year is a confusion of reds and golds,

but in the gulag of August
days are where you left them,

nights,
the same

19

Are you visiting the harems of April?
Travelling the great world of May?

Are you researching the archives of June?
Do the rains of July grieve you?

Are you saluting the landslides of August,
the independence of September?

Are you in unarmed combat with October?
Does November please you?

Is December your new best friend?
Are you hunting that grail, January?

Do you still have time for February?
Have you seen March,
celebrating the marriage of green and blue?

20

We were our own seraphs –
hours came and went
in the name of the east

All trees were the product of our love,
every bit of woodland listened to us

Ours was the tabernacle of light,
the sun our sphinx of the air

We signed the electoral register
of our hearts,

voting ourselves into office
again and again

21

I've lived with your death for a year,
that despot death, that realist,

stunned,
as if I've just given birth to a foal,
or made an enemy of the rain

All at once
you had more important things to do
than to live

Death is the feather in your cap,
the source of your fame,
my darkest lesson

This dropout year closes,
I begin my second year without you,
just me and the paper-thin world

22

The TV asks me,
how long after being widowed
before you start dating?

When China tours the world
by rowing boat,

when India is small as Ireland,

when that unbeliever water
turns to wine

23

I'm letting go of you
year by year

Today it was 1970,
tomorrow it may be 1977

There is so much of you,
you will never completely cease,

but slowly
I'm releasing some of you from me,

there's no rush, no deadline,
time doesn't matter,

its just that I can't despair forever

so I pour you away from me,
libation by libation,

as if discarding the water
from the font at Manaccan
in which an infant has just been baptised.

24

A world's daylight was not enough to keep you here,
nor the night's secret of success

Summer will never forget you,
nor friendly autumn

They'd stop at nothing
to keep you where you belong

Every afternoon reads between the lines
for news of you

and on the spur of the moment
evening welcomes you, who are never there

Next week knows his fatherland is too small for you,
and next year knows it too

No city working till late at night could keep you,
nor the happy endings of the sea

The theatre sold-out every night couldn't hold you,
nor the long disobedience of the truth

Today,
who is a shadow of his former self,
lets you go,

and so do I,
all my schools closed for summer,
silent for weeks

Spider

A spider's capacity for work
and self-expression

Apsidal, nimble,
not seeking approval

Not needing to get a mention
on the *World's 100 Best Webs*

With your laity of flies,
cajolery's not your style

You just like working,
then   waiting,

close by your close-fisted silks

Poem

A poem stays awake long after midnight
talking you from room to room,

does not care that walls have ears,
las paredes oyen

A poem prefers tin to silver,
silver to gold,
gold to platinum

Every year
a poem tosses a young woman from the cliffs
to the rocky sea below

A poem accidentally sends the entire letter *f*
off to Florence

but keeps the letter *t*
in a matchbox, like a tiny contraband tortoise

Sometimes
a poem is your only daughter

busy and happy in the world,
China or Spain,
abundancia de riqueza

Like the partial Angel Gabriel
in Santa Sophia
a poem is half-gold, half-invisible

A poem will do things in England
she'll never do in France

It will take more than the ten thousand lakes
for which Minnesota is famous
to drown a poem

The poem pauses now and then
to look at nothing-much-in-particular

A poem likes scraping and burnishing
the prepared surface of the etching copper,

is frequently found note-taking copiously
from *The Fantastic Historia Animalium of the Rain*

A poem makes herself tiny as a waterbear
or a tardygrade,
a mite able to survive freezing, boiling,

able to go into suspended animation
for one hundred years, if need be

Bashō

Bashō
saw the birth of a fawn
on the birthday of the Buddha,

omen of such an auspicious nature
he had to spend
the rest of his life living it down.

On his last journey,
when spring came
he sold his winter clothes,

just as my daughter did,
three hundred years later,
as she travelled not in Japan

but north to south
down the long pounding heart of China.

January x 2

If I had a horse,
which I don't,
and some harness,
which I haven't,
and if I could harness
a horse, which I can't,

that would be good enough for January

*

January, Janvier,
Enero, Gennaio, Januar

A windjammer under reduced sail
A box of 1000 aspirational envelopes
delivered by Paul

Two new saucepans, one from Tesco,
one from Boots

A sky not yet ashen

A shadow clock diagramming the hours,
their grave serious Roman roads

Things You Can't Post
(Royal Mail leaflet)

No prohibited drugs,
no living creatures,
(pigeons make their own arrangements),
no explosives, matches, bank-notes
(unless copies of obsolete items),
no filth.

No cathedrals, no oceans,
no thunders, no lightnings,
nothing flammable and/or obscene.
No ghosts, no trains, no dry ice,
no life-size lighthouses.
No mortbois.

You may post hope
and slowly fading emotions;
biscuits, flowers.
You may post all the opposites of filth,
almost all the varieties of the fragile,
(No fragile filth).

You may post keys, you may post locks,
maps and all that which must not bend.

But by all means post concertinas,
violins, flutes.

You can't post Pathogens in Hazard Group Four,
museum corridors or false alibis,
air pockets, or the essence of Zen
or a comet or a moonbeam or a huge mirror
intended to be sent up into the sky
to reflect sunlight on the winter cities of Russia,

or filth.

You may post torn hair,
rent garments, a tape of sighs.
You can post displeasure and/or benediction,
send it by land, air or sea. You may post
a substance you know or believe to be
capable of prolonging life
indefinitely.

This item will be impounded. (Like filth).

You can't post anything infra-red
or that sharp; no ports of call
or rivers, however small.
You can't (remember) post me.
I can't post you.
But you may post as many kisses as you think necessary.

(Kisses are no longer regarded as filth).

But post nothing irretrievably precious.
Nothing that might act in real or apparent
defiance of gravity. Nothing
that might lead to the conscription
of all men between the ages of 16 and 45.

Nothing with its enormous forepaw raised in menace
and its head turned towards the observer.
Nothing that squelches.
Nothing that moans.
Nothing so shadowy it may not be grasped for delivery.

No feculence, no cloaca, no filth.

In Cornish

Owl is Ula
Star is Steren
Pyscador is a fisherman
Morrab is his coast
His rainbow is camneves
His door is darras
Mor is his sea
Lor is his moon
His ear is scovarn
His eye is lagas
His eyes are dewlagas
Blejen is his flower
His summer is haf
Hunros is his dream

There is more to his lost language
than can fit on a tourist teatowel

Ore

I was a veinstone rich in chalcocite.
I was killas tongued with granite.
I was the dark green tongue-point
deep down in Michael Herodsfoot Mine.

I was bright green crystals lining a hollow
in a lump of quartz veinstone.
I was snake-green crystals
in a cavity resting on blueish copper sulphate.

I was in the dump at Wheal Cock.

I was connelite.
I was needle-crystals of copper ore
of a garter-colour and transparent,
so small I was not to be distinguished

from a needle without a magnifying glass.
When seen, I was pointed,
made of four-sided prisms and two-sided pyramids
ending in a point.

I was bevelled crystals
of sea-green with ivory
and pigeon-blood clouds,
turquoise with ruby veinings,

I was of a milk white colour,
plumose, acicular and radiated.

I was intermixed
with mammillary copper ore,
all open green and red ore.
I was black magnetic sand.

I was down in Wheal Treasure.
I was tin.
I was down in Wheal Busy.
I was arsenic and uranium.

I was down in Wheal Leisure and Wheal Friendly.
I was silver and lead.
I was down in The Phoenix and The Great Work.
What was I?

I was useful, I was recoverable,
I was Work.

wheal: mine.

Learning to Drive

It's no surprise the steering-wheel's round,
nor that roundabouts favour the circle also,

it's no surprise my left hand
doesn't know what my right hand's doing

nor that the Asda car-park
is suddenly brimming with menace,

unjudgeable spaces and evil kerbs,

it's no surprise that what I like best is driving along in a straight
line

nor that what goes on in the mirrors
goes on in a far-off parallel universe,

no surprise that the road-signs are written in Sanskrit
nor that my instructor Dave

suggests we break for five minutes –
'I'll add it to the end of the lesson' –

rolls with meticulous untrembling fingers
a neat spunky little roll-up.

Footnotes

1. Squid.
2. The evidences.
3. Of the savour of flowers.
4. i.e. weasand.
5. i.e. the Ottoman empire.
6. i.e. sleep.
7. An antelope with twisted horns.
8. His plan to impose a tax on the city urinals.
9. Or broad-beaked.
10. Arcades with recesses.
11. i.e. lost their scent.
12. Who died at the age of 969.
13. i.e. the science of magnetism.
14. A pugnacious corporate strategist.
15. i.e. self-invented.
16. 'Old April'.
17. i.e. banana, not pineapple
18. Also billed as *Miss La Roche*.
19. Admiral Hawker's fleet at Spithead.
20. Part stag, part lion, part badger.
21. A kind of gem.
22. A cordial or restorative.
23. A child-musician.
24. Poland.
25. i.e. the ambition of occult philosophers.
26. Newton's niece.
27. i.e. about twenty-five miles.
28. Who had 700 wives and 700 concubines.
29. A bassoon player in London theatres from 1875 on.
30. Altars.
31. But took little part in politics of the day.
32. A decisive naval battle.
33. Wrongly attributed to Goethe himself.
34. i.e. botanist; here, God.
35. Defies clarification.
36. i.e. volcanoes.
37. i.e. lopsided.
38. Directions for numbering the sands of the universe.
39. Hairy.

40. i.e. in a room.
41. Lord Falmouth, 1707-82.
42. Intelligence.
43. Shadow.
44. i.e. while on honeymoon in 1912.
45. A small sort of cabbage.
46. Especially Luther.
47. Multiplying them by ten.
48. Inventor of the first practical diving bell.
49. 'Long may you sleep'.
50. A poem of over a million lines describing the destinies of Central Asia from the beginning of time.
51. Numerous medical uses of the pigeon.
52. i.e. mosquito net.
53. i.e. cosmo-chemistry.
54. i.e. *perverse lingering*.
55. Who set up a cross-country postal service in 1730.

Pluvialist

The rain historian
devotes a thousand pages of praise
to each monsoon

He pens
a stern critique of hail,
exposing hail's abuse of rain

He re-drafts a belligerence
against snow

But gives a benedictive
to the dewfalls of dusk and dawn

Inventing

Imagine inventing yellow...
                    M.R. RICHARDS

Inventing yellow, and its opposite number
Inventing the earth, but without a moon
Inventing my father...but where is my mother?

Inventing angels, but there are too many angels
Inventing apples and their ultimate destination

Inventing blue, to measure the distance from sea to sky
Inventing blue, because it is kinder than birds
and because it is an innocent science

Inventing an hourglass, out of sheer longing for miracles
Inventing a shadow, an act of unskilled labour
Inventing a guillotine, a humane act, the dead cheering their heads off

Inventing love, which must be done blindfold
Inventing time, by pretending to be the same age as my child
Inventing a brave face, for walking out your front door each day

Inventing marriage out of whispers, explosions, mazes and survivors
Inventing an hour, in which to kiss in turn sixty Master Fan-Makers
from the Fan-Makers Guild

Inventing sleep, because I can
Inventing blue again, because I must
Inventing autumn, by saying your name twice
Inventing silence, by talking to a blue monkey
Inventing a seahorse, and interviewing him about fatherhood

Inventing a cloud, with Spanish books on its altar
Inventing prosperity, in the form of the Virtuous Lady Mine

Inventing the Squirm-Neck Chilean Flamingo, just for fun
Inventing butterflies –
                    fauns, palm-kings, duffers, jungle-glories –
just as a precaution;

Inventing a door, for leaving
Inventing Paris, so he may be watched by Aphrodite and Eros

Inventing an ocean, in case I need one later
Inventing twilight,
              and gently pulling the garden through it

Inventing a waterfall,
              so our dreams will always be the same colour

Inventing red, and its shadow

Inventing a landscape, by turning into a tree

Inventing luck, but then changing my mind and un-inventing it
Inventing an eclipse, as promised
Inventing a world through which light constantly passes

Inventing today,
              and putting it in writing

But He

But he lived in all weathers,
the rains of a lifetime,
standing shoulder to shoulder

with his childhood,
placing the alchemical vessels
of his thoughts in the light

with such care, such skill
they gradually sweetened
and vanished

He was the natural simplification
He was the dusk of a double winter

A Verdi of the forest
composing in leaf

He was the pre-history
of the oasis,

one of the butterflies
clustered
around the shield of *Jeanne d'Arc*

Every autumn he loved to show me
the sun's priceless collection of maps,

tracing the rivers
and mountain ranges,
the oceans in their joys

Only at the very edge
of my thought
did I know he'd never been born

Local Saint

*Not much is ever known of a local saint and his or
her name often has a number of variant meanings.*

Many begin life as a waterfall
or a well.

Others never even visit their birth-place
and constantly change sex,

tending to marry posthumously
and have twenty-four children.

Some saints celebrate their feast days
on different dates and at different locations,

as if you or I were to give ourselves
several auxiliary birthdays,

and each saint specialises
in one or two hard-to-swallow moments.

Nectan, newly-beheaded,
carries his head home to his waterfall,

nonchalantly casting his no-longer-needed bonce
into the waters,

so now they heal.

The Child Mylor,
hand and foot hacked off by his un-avuncular uncle,

grows them back
with almost reptilian-replacement skill.

Of Julitta,
nothing is known except her beauty,

and Sithney?
He preferred mad dogs to girls.

Sea otters
often dried Cuthbert's feet

after he'd paddled and prayed all day
in the icy North Sea's tide-line,

while pre-menstrual Urith,
sliced to bits by her pre-menstrual stepmother,

all at once became a stream.

The place invents the saint then?
Bio-theology?
A way of letting water wear a halo?

The saint the discovery
of the person water is, or wants to be?
And so begins a saint's career?

Ask Fillan –
he who wrote all night of The Lord
by the 60-watt light of his shining saintly arm.

With acknowledgements to *The Celtic Year* by Shirley Toulson
(Element Books, 1993)

Peaching

To bring about a peach
To endow a peach –

Like a great sleeper
asleep in his own image

In his own order of sleep,
in the high torpor of peachskin

To establish
the stone valances of his kernel

To arrange his leisures,
juices and dulcitudes

To grace a peach in his repose
with absolute luck:

to leave him
to the work of his harvest,

to the piety of his ripening,
the joy of his squandrance

April

Eyebright April

taking its ill wind
from town to town,

from branch office
to branch office

Unfolding the emptiest lily,
the wettest rose

Folding it up again,
its unfoldable water,
its Holy Land hopes,

its shadow
speaking a beautiful Hebrew

Fountains and Gateways

Like a flood alert for twelve rivers
or the oldest library in the world

or like the tired hands of a thousand scribes
or the need of a small child to be mothered

or like a someone beautified by the Pope
or one who believes

(despite all the evidence to the contrary)
that women cyclists are an affront to morality

or like an eleven year old boy dreaming
he is the twelve year old daughter of a drowning man

or the earth casting its own shadow into space

Or like the wail of a child
snatched from the flames by his foolish mother,

his immortality forfeit,
torn from the rule of his divine nurse

Like the intelligence-gathering of a kiss
or kissing as a type of improvised mouth-cricket

or like an unfinished iceberg
or the lino-tough soles of a barefoot runner

or an x-ray of the sun
showing his fiery visceral segments to be like an orange,

violent acts of swirl
and ejected gasses and extended prominences of flame

Or like a ghost nation far from home
or a look of ludic malevolence from Jack Nicholson

Or *the triple definition of a timeless idea*
found in the first paragraph of a novel by Henry James

or the patterns and intensities of lightning strikes
recorded in one year in Alaska,

or the recent reappearance in the Ukraine
of 500 lost works by the Bach family

Or the acts and seasons of the rainbow

Like one outside crying to come inside
and one indoors crying to get out

or the cool customer by a natural well
or the shame of fish

or the understanding of a small coastal vessel
or the boy in Voronezh

to whom the poet gave a goldfinch,
or like fountains or like gateways. *Like that.*

Task

Here's your rain,
that specialises in you

Here's your fret of looking, your silvery silvern,
your year of song, worldly with light

Here's your heart, and all that it can do
What can it do?

Here's your *ange bon temps*,
your *ange mauvais*

Here's your thought,
clouds over mountains
honouring someone

Here's your summer, slowly passing

Here's your mouth, and all that it can do
What can it do?

Here's your fear,
its restive stubborn clockwork

Here's your dream, ex libris

Here's your hand, and all that it can do
What can it do?

Here's your lovely wilding
tall and shrewd and now in bloom

Here's your Mercredi,
your Vendredi,

your house, its ups and downs,
your sky, de día, de noche,
your world and all that it can do

What can it do?

My Book

My book's in seven languages
Seven forecasts bring me
a cloud wolf and his seven shadows.

Every day seven postmen
bring me your love letters
in a pleasance of seven sacks.

My life is like seven oases,
a delight of quenching, of green places
and bronze brooks.

Then seven footsteps bring me back to my senses.

Second Official Language of the Bride

To imitate horses, but in a pure way.
To acquire hooves, pure mane, sweat. To gallop, purely.
To imitate the cloud-perdu of a garden
by sparing the lily
and by pursuing charities
with the eagerness of a golden thistle.

To imitate the journey of a snail-coquette,
or to cast an eclipse adrift
in a small green stay-at-home boat
called *Casa Real.*
To grow up fast
by admiring a staircase,

and to imitate a year
by holding a mirror up to the sky.

To assemble a rose: *Rosa de cien hojas*
                             Rosa Amarilla
                             Rosa Trémière
                             Rosa Muscade

To imitate a daughter, her merits
and kindness: *una hija amada.*

To render an earlier marriage safe
by concealing it in the Carthage of an old painting.
To complete the longest day
by island duties, or by claiming
the affection of water.
To imitate the limbo of a pearl.

To preserve a hand, at the expense
of a finger.
To love anyone you please, by pure gendarmerie.
To sing, by pocketing a little glass door.
To invent many new colours from memory.
To imitate a garden, by the silent use of a solar system.

To rest,
by means as yet unknown.

Tavosow

The tongue retreated,
fell back to the Mên Amber, hid out

at Carrag-luz, took rough shelter
underground at Wheal Baldhu,

built itself a house of sand
at Jangye-ryn

The tongue curled up
for simultaneous safety at Degibna
and Gwelabose

Sang hymns at Landewednack,
prayed for sanctuary in the woods at Ellenglaze,

joked with the divers
as they sifted through the silver lode
of the King of Portugal's treasure ships

The tongue uttered its last words,
left them on maps and signposts

The land was its sole mourner,
inherited all its owr and arghans,

every tikkidew and skaw,
its papynjays and its moredh,

every skavell-groenek and koukow,
every kastell and all its golowjow,

every hanternos, every single sterenn

Cornish-English glossary: *tavosow:* native tongue; *Mén Amber:* balance stone; *owr:* gold; *arghans:* silver; *tikkidew:* butterfly; *skaw:* elder tree; *papynjays:* parrots; *moredh:* sorrow; *skavell-groenek:* mushroom; *koukow:* cuckoo; *kastell:* fortress; *golowjow:* lighthouses; *hanternos:* midnight; *sterenn:* star.

Après Un Rêve

In my Mother's Day siesta
I dreamed
a poet called me on the phone –

'I can't talk long, Penny,'
he said,
'there's a guy staying with me

who's very unhappy,
he's waited weeks for his girlfriend
to call, so he doesn't like me

using the phone,
but listen' –

Now he must be holding the phone
out to the room
as the unhappy guy plays the piano and sings –

Après Un Rêve –
far-off and faint, the most beautiful rendition
I've ever heard,

so beautiful that when he's done,
I just put down the phone in wonder
without a word

to the poet or his friend the singer.

Après Un Rêve: Song setting by Maurice Ravel.

Azúcar

I have my own sugar factory.
Sometimes profits are up, sometimes down.
I rely on trial and error, quite a lot.

Sometimes I forget about my sugar factory
for weeks on end. Then I remember
and feel happy again just running it –

orders despatched, the wages, the VAT,
(love those forms!),
yes, running it smoothly enough in my head.

It's not much to other people, perhaps,
but it means everything to me –
And it hurts no one, except me.

Dukedom

He folds me in his dukedom,
draping its commemorative hills and forests
round me, casting his dukedom wide
till he's down to his very last caprice.

He folds me in his septembers worked
in ivory silk, in his seascapes of living memory.
He wraps me in his dukedom
of windfall, goldfinch and peach.
He inflicts his dukedom on me like dew on a fountain,
like a year of consents,
like a lily merchant.

He brings me a list of colours ranked in order of sleep.

With a smile taken at random
from the world's stockpile, he unfurls
his meridians, temples and folios,
folds me in his coastline, refractive and just,
doubles round me
in a popular uprising of emerald and jade,
surprises me
with his momentous green democracy,
fields, pastures.

He demonstrates by storm the properties of his echoes,
by example the heaviness of his spiders.
He wraps me in his *art du bonheur*,
in his protocols and grammars,
his guilds of water, in the gallantry
of his mistakes, and in the diagrams of his purgation.

He shawls me in a déshabillé of orchards,
in the armour of his thoughts and bones,
encircles me
with his dukedom of doors, porches and portals,
its neighbourhoods of counterpoise, ellipse and hyperbola;

he flies about me
in circumnambient marvels,
wrinkles and smoothes his maps expectantly,
swathing me in views of bridges, sheepfolds, boundaries
and elevations:

he cloaks me in leisurely lakes shining from pillar to post,
in lunar versions of his dukedom,
then pulls me into the thistledown of his physics,
his atoms pulsing.

He also makes known to me his Concept of the Round.

He lures me with his sugar factories,
tempts me with the silence of his herbarium,
its perfume-chimérique.
He wraps me in his protégé clouds,
in his skies dark as the mica sunk in granite.

He fastens his dukedom
round my throat,
the weighty balsams of its silver and gold
exciting respect, a collar of pertinence:
he plaits his dukedom into my hair,
anchorages of ruby, scruples of pearl,
adorning me with all his inferior and superior mirages.

He whispers a thousand dowries in my ear,
testing my arithmetic.
He floats his shipwreck museums up to me
from the depths.
He ravels me into his dukedom's conchology.
He brings me a list of colours ranked in order of aimance,

his dukedom
minding its own business, he says...

draping its commemorative hills and forests
around me, casting his dukedom wide
till he's down to his very last caprice,

and must turn reclusive,
lie among his riches
no louder than his own lullaby,

his dukedom no bigger than a visiting card.

My Folding Bedroom

Like Pharaoh's Wife,
I unfold my folding bedroom

where we can sleep
hand to mouth

or simply kiss
the way plenty of weather

outwits the forecasting;
flash floods streaming

from west to east
in a region

whose annual rainfall
is normally carried around
in a thimble

Eclipse x 4

For the eclipse happens at times when the light is defective.

Takeover

The sky takes over,
the moon takes over

The moon and her shadow take over,
so does the earth,
all poised in their line dance

Their skills, survivals and synchronicities
take over,
this is their version of life minus the sun,

silent, dimmed, charmed, brief,
a change for the worse

Look away now

The sun rolls back into place,
vast solar suttee blazing again
Two minutes and fifty seconds? Nice try, moon

Eclipse, eclipsed

Eclipse eclipsed by cloud,
by rain

Eclipse rage?

Think of Bashō,
visiting the Kashima Shrine
for the famed rising of the full moon
and being frustrated by the rain

Such a long way to come only
to look at the dark shadow of the moon

As if moons and eclipses
chose to be hidden, veiled, absent,

too good for the likes of us,
even Bashō,
scribe to the world,

even he not admitted to marvels

Totality

Half-lulled,
      half-angered
            by the wash-out eclipse
going on
     under cloud-wraps,
           I'm wrong-footed by the dark
as the moon lid
      clicks into place
          A dark that's out of this world,
cosmic black joke
       such as
         one of Hardy's Immortals
would crack
      But is light or dark
         the punch-line?
Optimist cameras
      flash silver,
        taking pictures of black,
of cold,
    of the moon's ultimatum
       silencing
even the quack of commentary
        from
         local radio FM:
And it's beautiful,
      pure total dark
        that times itself exactly
then
  from its yin
     lets go free into the world again
pang
  after pang
    of brightening

68

The Bat of Totality
(for Jane Tozer)

Sombre eclipse, more Scriabin than Chopin
Tenebrous eclipse, more Bruckner than Ravel

A drag of silver over the sea's sky:
rain or moon shadow?

No one can tell,
yet when the brakes of the cosmic car tighten

to a standstill
we feel this unseen eclipse in our bones,

brains, hearts, genes,
as evident as if we saw it through solar filters –

Eclipse more inner than outer –

until the swoop of total dark,
longest two minutes of my life,

including any two minutes
of the hours I was in labour.

Near Helston, a lone bat woke,
skedaddled across a friend's field,

maybe thinking,
where are my mothers, my fathers and my brothers,
my sons and my daughters,

my kin and my matrikin,
all my affines?

The Descent

The plane begins its descent over Birmingham
in order to land at London,

liking, like me,
this long lingering glide down through clearing cloud

over the river I think I know so well
and now learn so much more of

by flying overhead,
river swanning through various greens

and numerous greys
of its domestic landscape;

I like circling
the stockstill reservoirs who gather up
in their gravelly cups and chalices

London's just-about-palatable drinking water,
happy to quench,
to know much about thirst,

just as they did all through my childhood

Six-Billionth Baby

Today sees the birth of the world's six-billionth baby.
By the time he's an old man

the car-parking nightmare of Falmouth
will be resolved

and I will be long-gone.

By the time the six-billionth baby
is an elderly ex-millionaire

or a one-time mayor of Bombay,
I'll be experiencing non-being.

Maybe the afterlife
will be disappointing as a cloudy eclipse
or unjust as the death of the Cornish tongue,

maybe lovely and ungrudging
as in my life
only your daughterhood shone.

Her Houses

Water
living in all her houses at once,
with her bee and her blindfold hare

Her working child The Moon
flies overhead, from Syria to Spain,
from Greenwich to Azerbaijan

Her doors are the study of ancient climates,
her beds the voluptuaries of their era

Her common princes
change colour and voltage constantly

Her favourite?
A cleric who is Pope everywhere
but Rome

Master Town

The town like a meteor
in its bespoke streets,

the marble of its slang,
its yellow cheer-up doors

Town
in its upright nutmeg light,

its chatterbox complaints,
its gardens swallowed-whole

by the sky

Sometimes the sea comes along
to muss the orchards,

then the sun is a snake in the grass,
the houses don't turn a hair

In every shadow
there's a verandah

In every attic
islands are blowing their brains out

The bath-houses give sleep to their beloveds
The town just pushes on with its sheikdom

Then a broadly-copper moon comes,
round and smiting

Delta

All weekend
  god works overtime
creating
  many new lakes
just by breathing
  on glaciers
He has nothing but truth
  to feed his water demons on
That,
  and a sense of indigo
when tinkering with water
  Not just lakes,
mind you,
  but dams and reservoirs,
weirs and canals,
  Thy Sandbar,
Thy unappreciated oceans,
  Thy Breath
flooding the delta,
  double-quick

One House

A little quickstar
   ringing clear
alone in the sky
   above the sleep-sound earth
The sea with all its shrimps,
   its violet coasts,
its necklaces carried lightly
   like proverbs
such as
   The tongue will take you
as far as Kiev, or,
   In summer remember winter,
or,
   Teag ew hydruk

A slumming blue-tail jay
   far from home
once-overs the urban woods,
   hacks from tree to tree
in The Dell
   like a knight trapped in a wineglass,
the woods that speak for themselves
   a minute from my door

The star, the bird and the sea
You know they all live in one house?

Teag ew hydruk: beauty is fragile.

September

(for Caroline Carver)

The leaf-watcher's month,
if she can bear to

The year changing its mind
voluble as an older bride

The month undergoing pears

September being also a floating classroom
for studying the great lakes

September,
who gives anyone who asks

a guided tour of the year,
the month who keeps all the year's promises,

leaf by leaf

Art of Vanishing

Your hand vanished first,
portrait of peasant life.

Your other hand followed suit,
unfurling, hairshirt of a snail.

Your arms simply floated away,
twin seaports named after flowers.

Who will hold me now?

In order to engrave their travels
on a cloud,
your legs left not a wrack behind.

Your torso preferred to be desert sand
blowing about in crescent-shaped storms,
an existence without intelligence,

your head and heart blazed to nothing
on the funeral pyre of an apple tree,
your eyes a mere opthalmology of ash.

You'd gone,
like that house at Porkellis
hurtling down an old mineshaft,

or a cosmonaut abandoning Mir;
brief summer leaving Gondal
or a village razed by its neighbours.

Somewhere, of course, you began again,
reappearing limb by limb,
your anti-exodus,

curious about yourself
as any pencil is
with the portrait it is made to draw.

But where? Where?

God as Pupil

God leans back from the world,
sighing,

as if learning French
and disliking it.

His accent makes everyone weep.

So in a suitable teaspoon
he scoops up some lightning,

his favourite medicine.

Voilà tout, folks, says God,
ascending to his azure places.

Grows Rich

The sky grows rich,
at once looks ten years older

Mountains grow rich
by adopting the collective bargaining
of forests

Sun blazes on and on
in his own small friendly way

Geography grows rich
by learning how far from the sea he is

Winter grows rich
by not noticing clouds

The sea grows rich by joyriding beaches

Fathers and mothers grow rich
slowly and with great difficulty

Stone grows rich,
makes a new will written in blood

Peru grows rich
by leoparding all its lions

The dead grow rich,
reappearing as ears of wheat
or bunches of grapes so large
it takes two or three men to carry each resurrection

Hell grows rich
and re-decorates

Heaven grows rich
and re-decorates

You and I grow rich,
like the old cave painters
working by firelight

Postcards

Death quietly washing his or her hands,
counting the stones of China,
the shoes of the world to come

Many thanks for your grief,
says Death,
for your cloud and your story,
says Death

scrawling postcards
of the sunset
to all his friends

And wish oh wish you were here

An Account

Thrift is the world's riches made small
but just as real

Instead of forests, one leaf
Instead of entire coastlines, one bay

To take a dozen steps is freedom
after a long lock-down

The prison cell is also a haven,
if given value

Our travels are felt to the quick,
though we seldom go further than a mile

Thrift makes you handle every coin
not as a miser
but as a prince whose revenues are boundless

Son

My youngest son
shoves his way through cloud,

spotless,
dear of him,
as a city in miniature,

his sunlit angels roughing it,
his weighing pans golden and empty,
his eggs still in one bright basket

He's off on his round trip,
Alejandro Magno to the life

He's leaving,
for he's the dawn,
my good luck and my bad

The Town at Dusk

The town and all its waters
in a lock-up of mist, the bittern boom
of the lighthouse its only endearment

The dogs of the road go home
with bared eyes of fortitude

The homesick town pours scorn
on its twin's name

Wild is the book that holds it,
its melancholy, its watermeadow, its pining

Time-maker

The day went on making clocks and watches,
seeking absolute accuracy

I could do nothing about it,
though every second cried for mercy

In my own minute
I ventured and wept

In my own hour
I escaped and was re-captured,

in my own day
went through our homegrown rooms

that ticked and chimed
and struck without mercy

Town of Lost Farms

This is the town of lost farms and lost Jews,
of ships of other days

and streets straying from the flock.
This is the town of ancient war-like libraries,

of butchers' calm with listening,
windows of young twisting salmon.

Here's a town bright as a lost sword
or stretched like a stroke of dark paint
over the sky,

town with a tongue of myrrh,

town for every *estación*,
water-tight spring,

its winter all *espíritu maligno*,
autumn throwing in the towel,

only summer promising everyone whatever they want.

For an account of the once-flourishing Jewish community in Cornwall
see *The Lost Jews of Cornwall*, edited by Keith Pearce and Helen Fry
(Redcliffe Press, 2000).

Connecting House

I'm in an archaeologist's tent,
my connecting house

I'm here to learn English
Several women are tending a rose

Will it survive?

My tent is a tapestry of reds
and dark reds,

in this life I'm a virgin of 55
and the best ten nights of my life

are being spent watching a moon
rest her big light on one leaf

Eye-dog

I flow through your veins
and reach your heart –

it is the circulation of me

I climb the Alps of you,
I'm your view of Rome

My coinage is yours,
whether you count it or not

My bones
include themselves in your anatomy

My roof, walls and floors
build the house of me around you,

the furnishing of it is far from finished
Nor is it a firetrap

Beginning with a single thread of me
I'm spinning a made-to-measure cloak

to protect you
and all the strings of your bow

Like an eye-dog
I'll keep the hunters of you at bay

forever

Weather, Continued

I looked forward to the sky,
and working for myself

I was in full swing,
cloud by cloud,

no savant, no,
but I took my chances

Trees slowly filled up with light
beside my very-early path

I was prepared for noon's budding silence,

I'd converse with anyone
for the sake of my health,

like a young pearl,
or a long and rivered verse from Scripture,

or a tongue kept purely for singing

Fear

I drown water
I make ice shiver

I silence silence,
I darken darkness

I dry out the desert
and poison venom

I eclipse the eclipse,
I shock electricity

I execute death
I memorise memory

I pursue pursuit
and ask asking

I question questions
and listen to listening

I set firc on fire,
burn up the sun

I slow down time
and time speeds up

as only he knows how

The Glimpse

Everyone will be alive, but different,
some bright and fast as humming birds,
others slow as the beginning of rain.

But everyone will be a powerhouse,
some remembering love,
others not.

Everyone will be outspoken,
some will go on telling lies, others
will make up the truth, regardless.

No one will be rubbish,
or yearn for particular rivers,
as they did long ago.

Light will pour down its wild rays,
shadows rise up, scarlet and tall.

The Interior

All our lovely forests
have been taken away,
and our ice-cold lakes
to which no one needed to add
a finishing touch,
our fields also, cancelled,
green and local,
and our hills drawled-over with cloud;
as for our missing river
no one has seen or heard
a thing,
only the river's passport,
thrown aside,
all we have left is the sky
leaping lightly from day to night,
we keep close watch on it,
not even its tempests give us hope,
its darkest twilights occupy us for hours

Far

Far as I was
from rain or river,

from sky or school,
from each state-of-the-art tree

Far as I was
from day or night,

from star or sea,
from voice or touch

Far as I was
from Rembrandt and Van Dyke,

from any cloud,
lake or light-strewn city

Far as I was
from Africa or Antarctica,

from sleep or solace,
from my paperless office,

from rhyme, from reason,
from word, from mouth,

from this or that,
from you

or my lost and war-torn father

The World

When you're so tired
you can't bear the world,

that's when you really begin to live,
when you're closest to the world

How difficult it is to love it,
unlike the moon at first light

carrying her weight so readily
But the world

longs for all it will never have again,
that's the world's heavyweight nature,

all its mountains have fear,
all its chasms have sadness

In rainy weary prime of life
the world endures its broad lawful wings of light,

not beautiful, not happy,
so tired you can't bear it, how the world is.

Miedo

Fear has no last name, no first name,
is anonymous

in all the world's 8000 identifiable languages

Fear stamps his head on all coins,
stares over the golden rim,

knowing what he will see

Fear makes you see right through the world,
thins it out
till even the greenest leaf is colourless,

every blue flower foregoes its blue,
roses deny the reality of red

Miedo: Spanish for 'fear'.